My Invisible Friends

By Michelle Whitedove

Illustrations by Linda Poynter

WHITEDOVE PRESS

WHITEDOVE PRESS
C/O Book World
1941 Whitfield Loop Rd.
Sarasota, FL 34243

www.MichelleWhitedove .com

To order additional Copies of this book 1-800-444-2524

Illustrations by Linda Poynter

Book Design by ColorCraft 954-345-1002

Poem by Maliena Slaymaker

Printed on Acid Free/Recycled paper

Library of Congress Control Number: 2005923277

ISBN# 0-9714908-4-8

First Edition

10 9 8 7 6 5 4 3 2 1

Angels and Us

God created human souls and that's you and that's me,
And we were meant to visit Earth to see what we could be.

When God made humans, it wasn't for show,
It was so that each soul could learn and grow

In Heaven the angels spoke to you one day,
And asked if you'd come to Earth to play.

You looked at many families and God said, "Choose one."
But there were so many, it wasn't easily done.

Finally you did it. You chose your life,
And cherubs in Heaven sang to you of beauty and strife.

The angels in Heaven watch you on Earth learning new things,
And if you fall down you can land on their wings.

Because your invisible angel is God's helper and can intervene,
Even if they can't be seen.

-Maliena Slaymaker

Since the beginning of time, little souls just like you and I looked down from Heaven to see the beautiful Earth. Excited by all the opportunities, our angels ask us if we are ready for a big adventure.

We will leave our real home in Heaven and travel to Earth. With our angel's aid, they help us prepare for this special journey.

The families that we are born into are very important for our soul's growth, so with God's help, and the angels, we decide on parents and where we shall live.

All of the little souls get so excited about their journey to Earth. We make many plans for our future as we look in on our new families. We love them so much! But how will we behave with this family? Will we be good and stick to our plans? Who will we become when we grow up? How will we help other people? We make a promise to God on how we will conduct ourselves and what tasks we will try to accomplish. We make a long list of things to do. God calls this our contract.

Sometimes we forget about this agreement, but it is still there, deep down in our memories. We have many goals to achieve during our lifetime.

Once our plans are finished, there is a celebration in Heaven. Angels sing at this big party. Their songs radiate throughout paradise and you will feel all the love and support from your heavenly friends.

There is a reward for going on this journey. We are given an opportunity to come here to learn spiritual lessons to grow. The angels tell us that we will not go on this trip alone. We will have friends called Guardian Angels that will come with us, but they will be invisible to most people. Can you see them? Even if they can't be seen, most of us can hear our angels. They are the small voice inside us helping to give us direction.

When your soul comes into this world, you enter into a physical body but you still keep your heavenly spirit inside. You are born pure and good. Each soul arrives smelling of the fragrance of heaven. Have you ever noticed that special scent of a new born baby?

We come to Earth excited to meet our new families and begin an important adventure.

We are never alone. God assigns us two Guardian Angels to stay with us on Earth. These invisible friends help us throughout our lives. They inspire us, protect us, and guide us to fulfill our promises to God.

Babies often see their angels smiling and laughing with them. As you grow to be a toddler, you may continue to see your angels and recognize them as your invisible friends. Parents usually don't see our angels, but they should encourage this bond.

God and your angels are watching over you. They are your unseen support team. These invisible friends help to keep you from danger through their loving acts and encouragement.

Guardian Angels love us unconditionally. They can protect us from harm and will intervene when necessary. They are at God's command.

We can talk to our angels and God through our prayers. Our prayers are our words, our intentions, and our thoughts. These prayers are seen as beams of light going up to the heavens. Everything that we say and do, especially good deeds, is a prayer to God. It is important to talk to our invisible friends.

Many Children are aware of their invisible friends. They play with their angels, keep them company, and talk with them just like they are best friends. Children even give names to their angel friends.

ntuition is how God and angels communicate with us. It is important to listen to the little voice inside that gives us ideas and inspires us to be the best person that we can be. That voice comes from our unseen support team which is always looking out for our best interests.

Around the age of eight, many children stop seeing their invisible friends. An adult may have told them that it is just their imagination and that their invisible friends don't really exist. But God's truth does not change with our beliefs. God's truth is always the same. Angels do exist and are always with us.

Even when we are afraid because we think that we are alone, angels are always with us. They send us their love, prayers, and light.

Just use prayer to call on your angels for help. Prayer is how we talk to God and our invisible friends. They can hear our prayers whether we say them out loud or silently.

When we fall asleep at night our angels talk to us. This is the time that we are most open and able to hear them. Sometimes we even remember these conversations as dreams when we wake up. If you write down your dreams as soon as you awaken it may help you remember them later. Are there any hidden messages? Dreams are just another way that your angels communicate with you. Remember that you are never alone.

Sometimes our invisible friends talk to us through our thoughts or feelings. This is called intuition. Using your intuition is helpful when you are choosing friends or need help in making a decision.

We should listen to our intuition which is our inner voice. It's the voice of God and our Guardian Angels that helps us make better choices, whether it is about a person or a place. God assigned us angels so that we are never alone through life and so we always have the best guidance and counsel. They also give us unconditional love and comfort when we are angry, sad, and hurt.

Angels show us how to treat one another, which is always with love and kindness.

Meditation is another way to connect with your angels and the voice of God. Mediation works best when the mind and body are quiet. Find a peaceful place to be still and listen. A silent walk in nature is a wonderful way to meditate.

When we meditate, we are taking time out of our busy day to stop and listen to that little voice within. With practice we can learn to shut out all of the noise around us and hear what God and our angels are saying. Meditation is listening and praying is talking to our unseen support team.

Just like you, parents, grandparents, and even teachers, all have Guardian Angels that stay with them throughout their lives. Because we are loved equally, God made sure that we would have these angels as our unseen support team. Their number one job is to help us through each and every day. They do this by warning us of danger, guiding us to the right path, and helping us to celebrate every success in life.

Guardian Angels are your best friends.

This book is dedicated to:

My Guardian Angels who have worked
overtime protecting and inspiring me.

To all the children who recognize their
invisible friends and to those who believe
without even seeing them.

And to the parents of these children who
are advanced souls. Listen to your children,
in many ways they are your teachers.
These children are brave souls who
volunteered to help humanity.

In Love and Light,
Michelle Whitedove

Author Michelle Whitedove

with Pookie and Foxy

www.MichelleWhitedove.com

Illustrations by Linda Poynter.
For custom spiritual portraits like the one above, go to:
www.LindasARTrealm.com

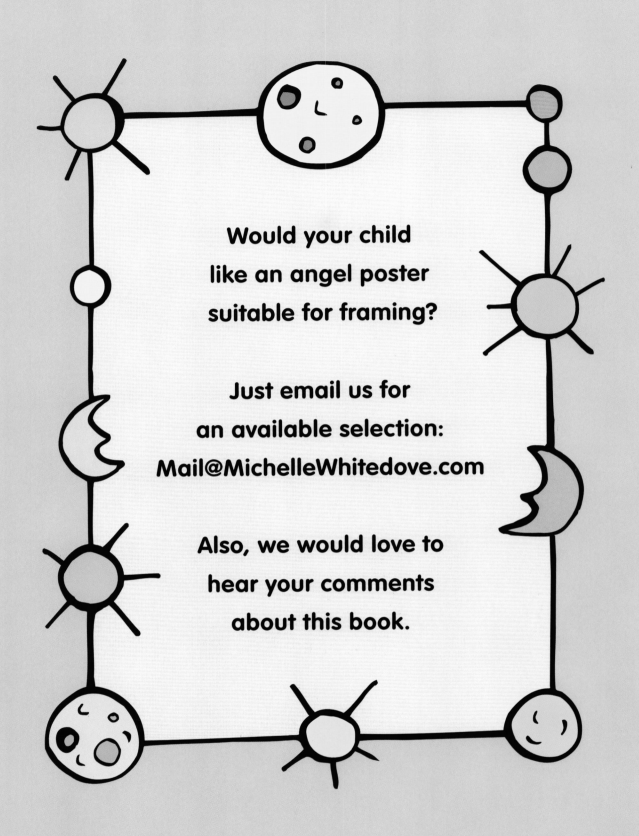

Would your child
like an angel poster
suitable for framing?

Just email us for
an available selection:
Mail@MichelleWhitedove.com

Also, we would love to
hear your comments
about this book.